GW01373143

FOR A GREAT FISHERMAN WHO HAS EVERYTHING

A Funny Fishing Book for Fishermen

Team Golfwell and Bruce Miller

For a Great Fishermen Who Has Everything by Bruce Miller and Team Golfwell

FOR A GREAT FISHERMAN WHO HAS EVERYTHING, A Funny Fishing Book for Fishermen, Copyright © 2022, Pacific Trust Holdings NZ Ltd. All rights reserved for the collective work only. No part of this book may be reproduced or transmitted in any form or by any means, electronic or mechanical, including photocopying, recording, or by any information storage and retrieval system, without written permission from the author, except for brief quotations as would be used in a review.

This is the seventh book in the series, *For People Who Have Everything, fka For Someone Who Has Everything.*

Cover by Queen Graphics. All images are from Creative Commons or Shutterstock

ISBN 9798435579888 (Amazon paperback)

ISBN 9798435709612 (Amazon hardback)

ISBN 9781991161673 (Ingram paperback)

ISBN 9781991161680 (Ingram EPUB)

ISBN 9781991164100 (Ingram hardcover)

For a Great Fishermen Who Has Everything by Bruce Miller and Team Golfwell

I told my wife I had to stop at the bank.

But I didn't tell her which one."

Catfish noodling is an unusual fishing technique used around the world. Fishing has been going on for thousands of years around the globe. Catfish noodling doesn't require a rod, reel, or any bait since you use your hand. It is ancient and was practiced by North American Indians. It is popular throughout the Southern states and along the Mississippi River.

When a catfish nests, they stay in a hole and you stick your arm in front of the catfish hole and down a Catfish's throat and drag it out of the water, using your hand as the hook. In other words, the noodler places their hand inside a discovered catfish hole to catch the fish. [2]

It is legal in Texas and West Virginia but has been made illegal or there are restrictions in several Sothern states since dragging the catfish out leaves their eggs unprotected and reduces the catfish population. [3]

Doctor. A small-town Doctor was infamous in the area for always catching unusually large fish. One day while he was on one of his frequent fishing trips, he got a call that a woman at a neighboring farm was giving birth.

He rushed to her aid and delivered a healthy baby boy. The farmer had nothing to weigh the baby with, so the Doctor used his fishing scales.

The baby weighed 21 lbs. 13 oz.

Tangled lines. Certain things show your character, and most fishermen know how anglers handle a tangled line reveals their true character.

"Give a man a fish and you feed him for a day.

Give a man another fish and he will be, like, "fish, again?"

The best conversation. Sitting quietly in total silence fishing with a fishing buddy makes you feel it is one of the best conversations you've ever had.

For a Great Fishermen Who Has Everything by Bruce Miller and Team Golfwell

Cutting the grass or fishing? "Three-fourths of the Earth's surface is water, and one-fourth is land. It is quite clear that the good Lord intended us to spend triple the amount of time fishing as taking care of the lawn."

    -- Chuck Clark

Give a man a fish and he will eat for a day.

Teach him how to fish, and he will sit in a boat and drink beer all day.

Remembering Ted Williams. "One guy that I wish was here right now is Ted Williams. He helped me so much, our long talks, not about hitting but about fishing, one of Ted's passions, and I wish he was here today to share this with me because I owe so much to Ted Williams."

    -- Wade Boggs

New at ice fishing. Two men from Puerto Rico visited Minnesota on a business trip and wanted to try ice fishing. They stopped at a bait shop near a frozen lake and went to get some supplies.

"We need an ice pick," said the first man.

The clerk handed them their gear and wished them happy fishing.

A couple of hours later, the second man came back and said, "We need another ice pick."

The clerk sold him the pick, and the man wandered off.

An hour later, both men walked into the shop again. They stormed up to the counter and said, "Ice fishing's terrible and the ice picks don't work. We want our money back!"

The clerk looked confused and asked them, "What's the problem? Are you not having any luck?"

Furious, the first man replied, "Of course not! We don't even have the stinkin' boat in the water yet!"

Cuban terrace. "I'm a Hemingway fan, so in a manner of speaking, I've been fishing with him already. But man, would I love to board Pilar in Key West and head south until we have a day-long battle with a tarpon, haul that bad boy up, then celebrate by telling lies over rum on a Cuban terrace."

--Marcus Sakey, American author, and host of the Travel Channel show Hidden City.

Roosterfish. The east coast of Costa Rica is known for its excellent tarpon and snook fishing. The west coast of Costa Rica is known for its excellent Roosterfish, Marlin, Snapper, Sailfish, Dorado, Wahoo, Tuna, and many more. Tales of catching a Roosterfish (which are also found on the west coast down from Mexico to Peru) are highly exciting.

One angler opined, "Roosterfish are one of those species that can get you hooked from the first time you see them. They're unlike anything else out there. Their wild mohawk and blue shimmer scream for a camera. Try catching one, and it's the reel that starts screaming.

"Roosterfish fight hard and don't give in easy. The way they move is erratic, bordering on berserk. They have enough power to break your line and burn your drag if you're not careful. They're made even more interesting by the fact that you can't catch them in the US. It's easy to see why some anglers spend their lives chasing Roosters around Central America." -- Albert.

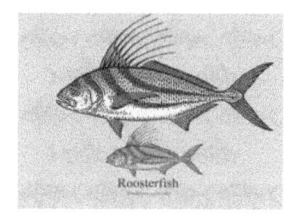

Roosterfish

Old fish. Did you know the orange roughy can live more than 150 years? [4] "The orange roughy is a predatory species that lives on deep seamounts (undersea mountains) in most ocean basins around the world. This species, also known as the Atlantic roughy, is one of the longest living marine fish species, with some living for more than 150 years. This longevity, and its other life history characteristics, makes the orange roughy vulnerable to overfishing." [5]

Fish not biting. A positive view of these times is best described by an old fisherman who expressed an opinion that he enjoyed the times when the fish weren't biting for then he had time to see and hear all the things he would miss if he was busy hauling in fish.

World's oldest goldfish. "Tish" is the world's oldest known goldfish and reached the age of 43. In the later years of his life, Tish faded from his natural bright orange to a more distinguished silver.

His owner said the secret of Tish's long life was not being overfed and being placed in the sun occasionally. Tish was won at a fun fair in the UK.

Save the goldfish! True story. A lady shop owner in the UK, aged 66, has been selling pets and fishing tackle for years from her shop in England. The laws there prohibited selling goldfish to a minor.

One day an officer from the trading standards department decided to lure her into selling a goldfish to an underage boy.

To most, it's not unreasonable for a 14-year-old to buy a goldfish. It is easy to understand the police setting up 'sting' operations for shops selling cigarettes or booze to underage youths, but it was reported the police spend and perhaps waste time and money on operations to trap shopkeepers selling goldfish?

Supposedly, a shop owner was caught selling a goldfish to a 14-year-old and the shop owner was fined 1,000 pounds. Believe it or not, the shop owner had to wear an electronic tag and was made the subject of a curfew order normally reserved for violent repeat offenders.

The PR department of the police announced, "Let this conviction send out a message that we will not tolerate those who cause unnecessary suffering to animals. We will not hesitate to use our statutory powers."

It was reported the goldfish was adopted by an animal welfare officer. [6]

When he's not talking football… "I can really fish - I've been fishing since I was a kid.

-- Deion Sanders, retired NFL player, and commentator.

No eyelids. Most fish don't have eyelids. Sharks are the only fish that have eyelids. Other fish have special eyelids that are thick and transparent, or see-through. Scientists think these special eyelids are a lot like glasses because they help fishes focus on objects. [7]

Obvious. Did you ever realize that if you took all the fish caught in Canadian waters during the past year and laid them end to end, there would smell very, very bad?

For a Great Fishermen Who Has Everything by Bruce Miller and Team Golfwell

Political discussion. Two men were out on a sportfishing charter boat in the southern part of the Gulf of Mexico between Cuba and Florida and got into a heated discussion about what political system is best. "Cuba is communistic, and they have survived happily for many years," one of them said.

The other man maintained, "Capitalism is far better since the Cubans have no incentive to improve their lives and a man needs to profit from his labor and not give it to the government.

Another fisherman overhearing this said, "Socialism is the best because it is based on sharing the wealth and the welfare of all."

Another said, "The entire world economy is complicated and overly confusing because of these different political systems."

The captain had heard enough and stepped in and said, "The world economy can be explained with two cows."

"How's that?" one of them asked.

The captain began, "With socialism controlling the world economy and you have 2 cows, you give one to your neighbor.

"With communism, if you have 2 cows, the State takes both and gives you some milk.

"In fascism, and you have 2 cows, the State takes both and sells you some milk.

"If you have too many bureaucrats or are in a bureaucratic society, and you have 2 cows, the State takes both, shoots one, milks the other, and then throws the milk away.

"Under capitalism, say you have two cows, you would sell one and buy a bull. Your herd multiplies, and the economy grows. You sell them and retire on the income.

"Under venture capitalism, and you have two cows. You sell three of them to your publicly listed company, using letters of credit opened by your brother-in-law at the bank, then execute a debt/equity swap with an associated general offer so that you get all four cows back, with a tax exemption for five cows.

"The milk rights of the six cows are transferred via an intermediary to a Cayman Island Company secretly owned by the majority shareholder who sells the rights to all seven cows back to your listed company.

"The annual report says the company owns eight cows, with an option on one more.

"Okay captain, we get what you mean. A corporation would be much better to run the world economy and be more efficient," one of them said.

The captain continued.

"If American corporation took over the world economy, and you have two cows, you sell one and force the other to produce the milk of four cows. Later, you hire a consultant to analyze why the cow has died.

"If a French corporation took over and you have two cows, you go on strike, organize a riot, and block the roads, because you want three cows.

"If an Italian corporation took over and you have two cows, and you don't know where they are, you decide to have lunch.

"If a Swiss corporation took over and you have 5,000 cows. None of them belong to you, but you charge the owners for storing them.

"If a Chinese corporation took over the world economy, and you have two cows, you have 300 people milking them. You claim that you have full employment and high bovine productivity. You arrest the newsman who reported the real situation.

If an Indian corporation took over, and you have two cows, you worship them.

"If a British corporation took over the world economy, and you have two cows, both are mad.

"If an Iraqi corporation took over, everyone thinks you have lots of cows. You tell them that you have none. Nobody believes you, so they bomb the crap out of you and invade your country. You still have no cows but at least you are now a Democracy.

"If an Australian corporation took over and you have two cows, business seems pretty good. So, you close the office and go for a few beers to celebrate.

"If a Scottish corporation took over and you have two cows, the one on the left looks pretty good.

"Finally, if a Greek corporation took over you would have two cows loaned to you by French and German banks. You eat both. The banks call to collect their milk, but you cannot deliver so you call the IMF. The IMF loans you two cows. You eat both. The banks and the IMF call to collect their cows/milk. You are out getting a haircut."

No deduction. "The gods do not deduct from man's allotted span the hours spent in fishing."

    -- Babylonian Proverb

Small rod big fish story. In Madeira, southwest of Portugal, a fisherman spotted a large blue marlin. Caught off guard and not having a big-game fishing rod handy at the time he spotted the huge fish, the fisherman grabbed light tackle with a 20 lb. line and caught an 807-pound blue marlin. [8]

Despite the negative odds of landing the fish using light tackle, the fisherman won the fight after only a 70-minute struggle.

At that time, the International Game Fish Assn. listed as the current low lb. line-class record of a 714-pound blue marlin caught off Africa's Ivory Coast in 1990.

The way it happened was that the fisherman and crew were storing gear on their final run before going into port when they saw the huge fish swimming near teaser lures behind the stern. So, after grabbing the light tackle, he immediately cast a squid at the fish that took it.

Luckily, the marlin didn't dive to the bottom as they most commonly do and that might have made landing it impossible. The large marline instead stayed near the surface and leaped often, revealing its location so the boat could be kept close and pointed in the right direction to help him land it. [9]

Only objective. "If catching fish is your only objective, you are either new to the game or too narrowly focused on measurable results."

— David Stuver, Familiar Waters: A lifetime of fly-fishing in Montana

How small was it? There is a fishing skill in Japan based on catching small fish. The smaller the fish - the bigger the catch! The most sought-after prize is to catch a fish as small as the diameter of a one-yen coin. [10]

Catching small fish is an art in Japan (which is also the home of bonsai trees). Fishing skills are measured by how small the fish is. It's called, Tanago fishing, an ancient Japanese fishing method dating back to the times of the Samurai hundreds of years ago. Tanago are several species of a small freshwater fish, known as "bitterling."

It's not easy to catch tiny fish. Japanese bitterlings are usually caught on handmade bamboo rods called Edo Wazao. They use a very fine fishing line and a needle sharpened with a jeweler's diamond file under a microscope.

If you think about it, it is more challenging to catch (without using a net, of course) the smallest fish than the largest fish.

Ideally, Tanago fishermen want to catch a fish that can fit on their one-yen coin (about 20 mm or .8 inch and that is just slightly larger than a dime).

The rods they use are small but relatively large compared to the size of a fish less than one inch long. [11]

Liars? "All fishermen are liars; it's an occupational disease with them like housemaid's knee or editor's ulcers."

    -- Beatrice Cook, Author

When you gotta go. True story. A dad took his 4-year-old son fishing and they were catching trout and smallmouth bass. The boy told his dad he had to "go number two" and his dad told him to hold on while he reeled in his line.

Too late. His son was already going "number two" in the live well in the stern of the boat. They came home with brown smallmouth bass and trout that memorable day.

For a Great Fishermen Who Has Everything by Bruce Miller and Team Golfwell

Ten Trivial Fish Facts.

1. A biologist who studies fish is called an "ichthyologist."

2. The most poisonous fish in the world is the Stonefish. Step on one and you've got problems.

3. The more sardines that are placed in a can, the greater the profit as sardine oil costs much more than sardines.

4. Minnows have teeth in their stomach that help them to digest their food.

5. The sturgeon is considered the largest of all freshwater fish and some have weighed in at over 2,000 pounds.

6. Fish can get seasick when kept aboard a rolling ship just like people.

A connection. "Fishing provides that connection with the whole living world. It gives you the opportunity of being totally immersed, turning back into yourself in a good way. A form of meditation, some form of communion with levels of yourself that are deeper than the ordinary self."

-- Ted Hughes, Poet Laureate UK, and writer.

Q. How do you tell the difference between a jazz musician and a fisherman?

A. You ask them to say the word "bass"

Amazing things inside fish.

- A Dutchman leaned over the side of his fishing boat and his false teeth fell into the North Sea. He concluded they were forever lost, yet three months later another fisherman found the dentures inside the stomach of a cod.

- A businessman who lost his mobile phone on a beach was amazed when it turned up - in the belly of a giant 25 lb. cod.

- Another fisherman lost a blue-stoned class ring that had his name engraved on the inside of the ring while fishing in Lake Sam Rayburn, in Eastern Texas. The ring turned up inside an 8-pound bass 21 years after he lost it by another fisherman fishing in that lake.

- A gold ring turned up inside the belly of a fish caught by an angler off Fort Victoria, near Yarmouth, Isle of Wight, in the UK.

More than catching fish. "If I fished only to capture fish, my fishing trips would have ended long ago."

-- Zane Grey

Trout tickling. [12] Similar to catfish noodling, another unusual fishing technique is trout tickling, which seems to have originated in the UK. It has been going on for a long time as even Shakespeare mentioned it in his writings. It is difficult but if you master the technique, you again don't need a rod, reel, or any bait.

You spot trout and then rub the underbelly of a trout with your fingers. If done smoothly and casually, the trout will go into a trance after about a minute, then you simply pick it up and toss it onto the nearest bit of dry land. Check the current law before you try this as it is believed to have been declared illegal in the UK. [13]

For a Great Fishermen Who Has Everything by Bruce Miller and Team Golfwell

Honest? "Fly fishermen are born honest, but they get over it."

    -- Ed Zern

How can this be? It is reported that biologists at the University of Manchester, England, discovered three fish inside a sealed egg. These biologists found the duck egg in a small pond on a field trip to the French Alps and noticed it appeared to be moving because of something inside it. They cracked open the shell, three live minnows were inside. They have not figured out how this happened and are completely puzzled

Being an optimist. The pessimist fisherman says on a stormy day, "This weather is terrible, and it can't get any worse! And the fishing is terrible, and it can't get any worse. Your boat is starting to stall out. This whole trip just can't get any worse."

Optimist fisherman replies, "Yes it can."

Vice versa. Give a man a fish, and he'll eat for a day.

Give a fish a man, and it will eat for weeks!

    -- Toshihiro Kawabata

Fine line. There's a fine line between fishing and just standing on the shore like an idiot.

    -- Steven Wright

End to a means. "The only reason I ever played golf in the first place was so that I could afford to hunt and fish."

    -- Sam Snead

Golden rule. The fisherman's golden rule: the one that got away is always bigger than the one you gotta weigh.

    -- Anon.

Rays can be troublesome! An angler in the UK supposedly landed a giant stingray while freshwater fishing. It weighed 770 lbs. and took about 90 minutes to land, and 13 men to heave it out of the water. It was 7ft long with a tail of 10ft. It was released unharmed after being measured. The man who hooked it was completely exhausted, then had a cold beer. [14]

Snapped the rod – the one that didn't get away. Dad was fishing off his son's dock in Florida and got snagged. The dad reported,

"I couldn't feel any movement. I was trying to pull the line free. Then my son came over and told me how to do it without breaking the rod and he took the rod and told me he could feel it moving and there might be something on the end of the line.

"I asked what it could be, and he thought it might be a ray.

"The water in the canal muddy because of mangrove roots, etc., and the sun was setting and getting dark.

"My son struggled to bring in the line and the thing started to move a little faster. So, I took the rod and immediately snapped it by pulling too hard. I felt bad and brought the line in hand over hand. And, after a few moments, through the dark murky water, I saw a huge mouth wide open coming up fast. I started to back away, not knowing what I was getting into.

"The next thing I heard was laughter from my son. When the 'big open mouth' came out of the water, it turned out to be a five-gallon bucket half-filled with canal mud and debris. I had snapped his $200 rod and got all excited over a cheap plastic bucket of mud!

"Lucky for me the rod had a lifetime guarantee, so all I had to pay was shipping and handling. So, this is a story about the one that didn't get away."

3 words. There are three words fishermen love to hear, "Get the net!"

Bull sharks. Pound for pound, Bull sharks have more testosterone than anything alive on the planet. [15]

A school of bull sharks damaged the rear of a shrimp boat breaking its tail shaft leaving the boat and crew adrift about 100 miles off the Florida coast. Bull sharks had been following the boat for several days, eating food and catch discarded by crew, and chewing on the boat's shrimp nets. The captain guessed a large adult bull got caught in the propeller and broke the drive shaft. The crew was rescued two hours later by another boat, but the boat that was damaged eventually sank in waters having 6-to-8-foot waves. [16]

Old fashioned. "I am an old-fashioned angler seeking to fish in a peaceful and relaxing way in traditional surroundings. Other anglers are too noisy, too busy, and catch fish that might break my landing net."

— Fennel Hudson, Wild Carp, Fennel's Journal No. 4

Did you know fish communicate with each other? Fish don't have vocal cords. However, according to the SPCA, fish are excellent communicators by other methods.

"They accomplish communication through various sounds, scents, electrical pulses, and motions. For example, knifefish and elephant fish can send and receive electrical signals used during courtship, navigation, and hunting." [17]

Fishing dad jokes (for sharing with kids or grandkids)

Grandad and his grandson Billy are searching in the woods for fishing worms to use as bait. They come across many different insects but nothing suitable to use for bait until little Billy proudly holds up a long dangling insect.

Little Billy shouts out, "I found some bait grandad!" and holds up a withered noodle-like soggy leaf.

"Sorry Billy we can't use that. It's not an earthworm."

Little Billy replies "Well, what planet does it come from Grandad?"

*

Son: "Have you ever seen a catfish dad?"

Dad: "I sure have"

Son: "How does it hold the rod."

Q. What did people call the fish who went to medical school and became a surgeon?

A. A sturgeon.

*

For a Great Fishermen Who Has Everything by Bruce Miller and Team Golfwell

Q. Where do you think a fish would go to borrow money?

A. A loan shark.

*

Q. What is that woman's name that keeps catching fish?

A. Annette.

*

Q. Which country is the favorite holiday destination for fish?

A. Finland.

*

Q. What's a lazy crawfish called?

A. A slobster.

*

Q. Why are fish boots so warm?

A. They have electric eels!

*

Q. How did the fish get into medical school?

A. On a scallopship.

For a Great Fishermen Who Has Everything by Bruce Miller and Team Golfwell

*

Q. Which fish won the award for best dressed at the beauty pageant?

A. The swordfish because she always looks so sharp.

*

Q. What would you get if you cross an owl with an oyster?

A. Pearls of wisdom!

*

Q. What do fish say when they swim into a concrete wall?

A. Dam!

*

Q. What do you call a fish with no eye?

A. Fsh!

*

Q. How do baby and small children fish go to school?

A. They use the octobus.

*

Q. Why was the baby fish not sleeping?

A. Because the seabed was wet.

For a Great Fishermen Who Has Everything by Bruce Miller and Team Golfwell

*

Q. Where do fishermen go to get their hair cut?

A. To the bobber shop.

*

Q. What did the fisherman want?

A. A gillfriend.

*

Q. What did the fisherman do to fix the piano when it sounded off?

A. He got a piano tuna.

*

Q. What is the best way to communicate with a fish?

A. Drop it a line.

*

Q. If a fisherman invents complex high-tech gear to catch fish, what should he call it?

A. Artie-Fish-el Intelligence.

*

A fish was arrested and put on trial. After the trial proceedings, the fish was standing in front of the jury in court. The judge asked the jury, "How do find the fish defendant?"

The foreman of the jury stood up and said, "We find the fish to be gill-ty"

For a Great Fishermen Who Has Everything by Bruce Miller and Team Golfwell

*

Q. What did Dad (Granddad) say when everyone was getting annoyed at his fish jokes?

A. "I really should scale back."

Flashlight. There was a Kentucky country boy and an Ohio city boy, fishing on their respective sides of the Ohio River. Just as soon as the Kentuckian put his line in the water, he caught and slung a fish onto the bank.

The buckeye was catching nothing, so he yelled across to the Kentuckian, "Buddy, I'd sure like to be on your side of the river!"

"Aight, tell ya whut, I'll shine my flashlight 'cross this river, and you can walk across this little beam of light!" the Kentuckian yelled back.

The buckeye replied, "Hain't no way, buddy. I know you think I'm a fool! When I get halfway 'cross, you'll turn your flashlight off!"

Demagogue. A demagogue is a political leader who seeks support by appealing to the desires and prejudices of ordinary people rather than by using rational arguments.

The ancient Greek playwright, Aristophanes, wrote that "Demagogues are like the fishers for eels; in still waters they catch nothing, but if they thoroughly stir up the slime, their fishing is good; in the same way it's only in troublous times that you line your pockets."

— Aristophanes, Ancient Greek playwright.

Finding yourself. "Many men go fishing all of their lives without knowing that it is not fish they are after"

-- Henry David Thoreau

Definition of an angler. An angler is a man who spends rainy days sitting around on the muddy banks of rivers doing nothing because his wife won't let him do it at home.

-- Author Unknown

For a Great Fishermen Who Has Everything by Bruce Miller and Team Golfwell

Chumming around the world and fish tastebuds. Chumming is the blue water fishing practice of throwing ground bait called "chum" into the water to lure various marine animals (usually large game fish) to a designated fishing ground, so the target animals are more easily caught by hooking or spearing.

Chums typically consist of fresh chunks of fish meat with bone and blood, the scent of which attracts predatory fish, particularly sharks, billfishes, tunas, and groupers. In the past, the chum contents have also been made from "offal", the otherwise rejected or unwanted parts of slaughtered animals such as internal organs.

In Australia and New Zealand, chum is referred to as burley, berley, or berleying. In the United Kingdom, it is also known as rubby dubby (West Country and Yorkshire), shirvey or chirvey (Guernsey, Channel Islands), and bait balls.

Chumming is a common practice seen as effective by fishermen all over the world. Multiple forms of chum are available and used by anglers. Bunker consists of fish parts with a fish-enticing aroma. Stink bait contains oily fish parts and blood that releases the scent of dead fish into the water. [18]

Most fish have highly sensitive taste buds located all over the outside of their body. [19]

Fishermen can get very creative in what they use as chum. There are dozens of ingredients like rabbit food, rabbit pellets, cat food, dog food, pilchards, anchovy oil, bread, rice, ground mullet, rolled oats, menhaden oil, squid wings, clam juice, shrimp bullion, clamshells, black lugworms, fish meal, flour, bloody fish like mackerel or jack, stinky cheese, garlic powder, canned tuna, mussel shells, and the list goes on and on…

Fish are like women in a way. "If you want the most beautiful fish in the sea, make sure you have the most appealing bait."

— Matshona Dhliwayo

Puzzling. Why do we throw our bait toward the middle of the lake but throw our bait towards the shore when we are in a boat?

-- Anon.

Old sayings. Get your kids hooked on fishing and they'll never have enough money for drugs or alcohol.

-- Anon.

An elusive pursuit. "The charm of fishing is that it is the pursuit of what is elusive but attainable, a perpetual series of occasions for hope."

　-- John Buchan

Bait (just joking). A priest was walking along the cliffs at Dover when he came upon two locals pulling another man ashore on the end of a rope. "That's what I like to see," said the priest, "Men helping their fellow man."

As he was walking away, one local remarked to the other, "Well, he sure doesn't know the first thing about shark fishing."

More than fish. "Fishing is much more than fish. It is the great occasion when we may return to the fine simplicity of our forefathers."

　-- Herbert Hoover

Did you know how fish detect movement? (You probably already know this) "Fish have sensory scales along their body called the lateral line. These sensory scales can pick up low-frequency sound waves that vibrate through the water. So, it makes a lot of sense to drop an anchor as quietly as possible.

Also, salmon are known as one of nature's best navigators due to their sensory capabilities. Salmon return to the same river, and sometimes even the same riverbed, in which they were born to spawn. They are guided by magnetic fields and their keen senses. It's believed the salmon, who can smell chemicals down to one part per million, can detect pheromones that are unique to their home stream." [20]

Fish or talk. No one in this town could catch any fish except one guy. The game warden asked him how he did it. The man told the game warden that he would take him fishing the next day.

Once they got to the middle of the lake the man took out a stick of dynamite, lit it, and threw it in the water. After the explosion fish started floating to the top of the water. The man took out a net and started picking up the fish.

The game warden told him that this was illegal. The man took out another stick of dynamite and lit it. He then handed it to the game warden and said, "Are you going to fish or talk."

Drone fishing. Another unusual and modern technique is drone fishing where you send the drone out over the sea to locate fish. Once spotted you can move your boat to that spot or if you are onshore, you can send out a torpedo fishing device with a long line attached. Please check local laws as drone fishing is illegal in Australia and some US states.

Important. If people concentrated on the really important things in life, there'd be a shortage of fishing poles.

-- Doug Larson

Thirsty snake. A man went fishing one day. He looked over the side of his boat and saw a snake with a frog in its mouth. Feeling sorry for the frog, he reached down, gently took the frog from the snake, and set the frog free.

But then he felt sorry for the snake. He looked around the boat, but he had no food. All he had was a bottle of bourbon. So, he opened the bottle and gave the snake a few shots.

The snake went off happy, the frog was happy, and the man was happy to have performed such good deeds. He thought everything was great until about ten minutes later, and he heard something knock against the side of the boat. With stunned disbelief, the fisherman looked down and saw the snake was back with two frogs!

Why did I make movies? "I only make movies to finance my fishing."

For a Great Fishermen Who Has Everything by Bruce Miller and Team Golfwell

-- Lee Marvin, Actor

Unbelievable. A man came home very late to meet his very aggravated wife. "Where were you?" she demanded.

"Well, you see Honey I went fishing and thought I would just do a little bank fishing, got my gear out of the car, and walked a bit to the water. I threw my line in and oh boy I pulled in a big catfish.

I then realized I forgot to bring my fish basket. So, I just threw the catfish behind me under a tree. I baited up again and in a little while, I caught one of those dogfishes. I didn't want to put it back in the water, so I threw it under the tree too.

I baited up again and sat there waiting for my next catch. Suddenly, I heard such a noise and when I looked that dogfish and that catfish were in a fight and that dogfish chased the catfish up that tree and I had to sit there all day before I caught a swordfish to saw that tree down to get my catfish.

Evening prayer. "Thank you, dear God, for this good life and forgive us if we do not love it enough. Thank you for the rain. And for the chance to wake up in three hours and go fishing: I thank you for that now, because I won't feel so thankful then."

-- Garrison Keillor

Dad fish joke. Q. If an oyster met with an accident, how will you take him to the hospital?

A. In a clam-bulance!

Grandpa's experience. "Remember when your GPS and a fish finder were rolled into one trusty unit called 'grandpa?'"

Fishing vs. Women. You can catch and release a fish; you don't have to lie and make promises.

Fish don't compare you to other fishermen and don't want to know how many other fish you caught.

In fishing, you lie about the one that got away. In love, you lie to still be friends.

You don't have to necessarily change your line to keep catching fish.

You can catch a fish on a 20-cent nightcrawler. If you want to catch a woman that costs a minimum of a dinner and a movie.

"I fish because I love to . . . because I love the environs where trout are found . . . because I suspect that men are going along this way for the last time, and I for one don't want to waste the trip . . . and, finally, not because I regard fishing as being so terribly important but because I suspect that so many of the other concerns of men are equally unimportant—and not nearly so much fun."

— John Voelker, lawyer, author, and fly fisherman

Tigerfish tournament. [21] Tigerfish are considered one of the most dangerous fish in the world since they have razor-sharp teeth. They are large and voracious.

Creative Commons

Each year around October during the full moon there is a Tigerfish tournament on Lake Kariba (between Zambia and Zimbabwe in Africa). People get tigerfish crazy and come from all over the world for the Kariba Invitation Tigerfish Tournament (KITFT).

The tournament was started in 1962 is now considered to be the largest single-species four-man Fresh Water Fishing tournament in the world.

The biggest, the goliath tigerfish (Hydrocynus goliath), is among the most famous of the tigerfish species – the largest one on record is said to have weighed 70 kg (154 pounds) from the Congo River but the tigerfish in Zimbabwe are smaller and weigh around 10-12 kgs (Hydrocynus Vittatus).

Competing boats may not fish within 100 meters of another boat without an invitation. Fishing on the 3 days runs strictly from 6 am, and you need to bring your fish to be weighed at 4.30 pm on the dot. [22]

Fish on! "When the fish are biting, there's no problem in the world big enough to be thought about."

    -- Anon.

Grandpa's influence.

Grandson: "Daddy taught me how to fish but grandpa taught me how to CATCH a fish!"

Grandpa: "The most valuable catch is time spent passing along a tradition."

Fish shop. A woman rushes into a fish shop at 4:45 pm on a Saturday and orders a pound of salmon.

The shop owner says, "I'm sorry, we've sold out of salmon."

The woman says, "But I want a pound of salmon!"

The fish shop owner says, "I'm sorry, but we have sold right out of salmon."

The woman repeats, "But all the fish shops sell salmon!"

"I know, I know, but we have sold right out of salmon."

The persistent woman repeats, "But I want a pound of salmon."

The shop owner stops and thinks then says, "Let me put it this way, spell perch without the "P"."

The woman says, "e-r-c-h."

The fish shop owner says, "now spell salmon without the "F".

The woman says, "But there's no "F" in salmon."

The owner says, "Exactly madam."

Getting warm. The great white shark can raise their body temperature. This helps them hunt for prey in cold water. [23]

Father shark teaches. A shark is teaching his kid how to hunt and eat humans.

He says, "Look son, first you swim full speed at the human but at the last second, you turn away. Then you swim at him full speed again, but again at the last second you swim away. Then you can go back and eat the human."

The son looks confused and asks, "But dad, why don't we just go and eat the human the first time?"

Dad shark replies, "Well, you can, but they taste better if you scare the crap out of them first."

Silence is golden. Two men are quietly sitting in a fishing boat sucking down beers. The first man says, "I think I'm going to divorce my wife - she hasn't spoken to me in over 2 months."

The second man sips his beer and says, "You better think it over - women like that are extremely hard to find."

"**You can spend a lifetime at sea**. Your present and past surround you as sure as the salt air. One does not stare out to the horizon and eventually not see themselves staring back. The farther we go out to sea, the deeper we go inside our mind. The spirit of the ocean is a living, breathing thing, as alive as any of the creatures who inhabit her waters above and below."

— Kenton Geer, Vicious Cycle: Whiskey, Women, and Water

Fish poem.

Early to bed,

Early to rise,

Fish all day,

Make up lies.

Smallest fish in the world. There are around 20,000 different species of fish in the world. Scientists also believe there are probably 20,000 undiscovered species. [24]

As far as is known the dwarf pygmy goby is the smallest fish in the world reaching a length of nearly one-half inch in adulthood. They are found in the Philippines. [25]

More dad/grandpa jokes.

Q. What type of fish loves eating mice?

A. Catfish.

*

Q. Where do all the fish safely deposit all their money?

A. In a riverbank.

*

Q. What do you think a shark puts in a peanut butter sandwich?

A. Jellyfish.

*

Q. Why is it easy to measure a fish's weight?

A. Because they have their own scales.

*

Q. Which fish only swims at night?

A. A starfish.

*

Q. What supplements do fish take to stay healthy?

A. Vitamin Sea.

*

Q. What would someone call a fish with two legs?

A. A two-knee (tuu-nah) fish.

*

Q. Why do fishes swim in schools?

A. Because they don't have fish colleges.

*

Q. Have you wondered what a fish's favorite musical instrument is?

A. A bass guitar.

*

Q. Which fish was featured in the latest feature fishing movie?

A. A starfish.

Nature of Angling. "Angling may be said to be so like the mathematics that it can never be fully learned."

    -- Anon.

Definition of a fish. "Fish: An animal that grows fastest between the time it's caught and the time a fisherman describes it to his friends"

    -- Anon.

Excuse me. Hammerhead sharks can swim in large schools of more than 500 sharks. The strongest female swims in the middle of the school. When she is ready to mate, she shakes her head from side to side signaling other female sharks to move away so she is well noticed. [26]

For a Great Fishermen Who Has Everything by Bruce Miller and Team Golfwell

Born again. John was the only Southern Baptist person to move into a large Catholic neighborhood and Baptists generally do not recognize the Lenten season.

On the first Friday of Lent, John was outside grilling a big juicy steak on his grill. Meanwhile, all his neighbors were eating cold tuna fish for supper. This went on each Friday during Lent.

On the last Friday of Lent the neighborhood men got together and decided that something just HAD to be done about John, he was just tempting them to eat meat each Friday of Lent and they couldn't take it anymore. They decided to try and convert him to Catholicism. They went over and talked with him and were so happy that he decided to join all his neighbors and become a Catholic.

They took him to church and the priest sprinkled some water over him and told him "You were born a Baptist, you were raised a Baptist, and now you are a Catholic."

The men of the neighborhood were so relieved, now their biggest Lent temptation was resolved.

Then next year's Lent rolled around. The first Friday of Lent came and just at supper time when the neighborhood was setting down to their fish dinners came the wafting smell of steak cooking on a grill. The neighborhood men could not believe their noses! What was going on???

They called each other up and decided to meet over in John's yard to see if he had forgotten it was a Friday in Lent.

The group arrived just in time to see John standing over his grill with a small pitcher of water. He was pouring small droplets over his steak on the grill and saying, "You were born a cow, you were raised a cow, and now you are a fish."

I miss my boat. "At sea, I was the captain. I was important, and I had a role. I ran the show.

At home, I was the swab. I did the crap work, almost always unappreciated. I loved my family, but man did I hate being on land all the time. I tried my best, I honestly did. I really stepped up my game around the house to be the best dad and partner I could be. It just was never good enough.

With no offshore fishing and encouragement at home, part of me was dead inside, the part that made me who I am. I missed my boat daily. Flashbacks were a constant. I daydreamed of foaming schools of tuna while washing bubbly dishes. I saw mahi-mahi boldly charging baits as I folded brightly colored laundry. When I went jogging and my heart started pumping, I saw huge marlin going wild on the gaffs. Everything reminded me of the boat.

I most likely honestly had post-traumatic stress from the whole ordeal"

— Kenton Geer, Vicious Cycle: Whiskey, Women, and Water

More dad/granddad jokes.

Q. Why did the fish cross the road?

A. To get to the other tide.

For a Great Fishermen Who Has Everything by Bruce Miller and Team Golfwell

*

Q. Where are whales taken to be weighed?

A. To the whale-weigh station!

*

Q. What's a really smelly fish called?

A. A stink ray.

*

Q. Why are fish considered very smart?

A. Because they live in schools.

*

Q. What type of fish are found in heaven?

A. Angelfish.

Tiger. "I thoroughly enjoy getting away from the game and going out fishing because it's so relaxing, so quiet, and peaceful. I mean, there's no noise other than nature - and it's so different from what I do in a tournament situation that it just eases my mind."

    -- Tiger Woods

"Give a man a fish, he'll eat for a day.

But if you teach a man to fish... then he must get a fishing license.

But he doesn't have any money, so he must get a job and enter the social security system.

And he must file taxes, and you're gonna audit the poor s.o.b because he's not really good at math.

You pull the IRS van up to his house and take everything.

You take his velvet Elvis and his toothbrush, and it all goes up for auction with the burden of proof on him because he forgot to carry the 1.

All because he wanted to eat a fish, and he couldn't even cook the fish because you need a permit for an open flame."

– Doug Stanhope, Comedian

The Most Interesting Fisherman in the World. "I don't always tell people where to fish, but when I do, it's a lie."

Fishing license. A couple of young boys were fishing at their special pond off the beaten track. Suddenly, the Game Warden jumped out of the bushes.

Immediately, one of the boys threw his rod down and started running through the woods like a bat out of hell. The Game Warden was hot on his heels. After about a half-mile, the young man stopped and stooped over with his hands on his thighs to catch his breath, and the Game Warden finally caught up to him.

"Let's see yer fishin' license, Boy!" the Warden gasped.

With that, the boy pulled out his wallet and gave the Game Warden a valid fishing license.

"Well, son," said the Game Warden. "You must be about as dumb as a box of rocks! You don't have to run from me if you have a valid license!"

"Yes, sir," replied the young guy. "But my friend back there, and well, he doesn't have one."

Do fish sleep or just rest? According to the National Oceanic and Atmospheric Administration, it is more like fish simply rest. "The dictionary defines sleep as a recurrent period of rest in which the nervous system is inactive, the eyes closed."

But fish don't have eyelids (except for sharks) and many fish live motionlessly. "Most fish rest. Some float in place, some wedge themselves into a spot in the mud or the coral, some even build themselves a nest. They are still alert for danger, but they are also 'sleeping.'" [27]

More dad/grandad jokes for kids.

Q. Why did the baby fish want to become an astronaut?

A. Because he wanted to go to the trout-er space.

For a Great Fishermen Who Has Everything by Bruce Miller and Team Golfwell

*

Q. Why are goldfish always orange in color?

A. The water makes them rusty.

*

Q. Why are fish considered gullible?

A. They have a habit of falling for hooks and sinkers.

*

Q. What did the fisherman say to his friend while fishing?

A. He was feeling fin-tastic.

*

Q. What will you get if a fishing rod is crossed with a gym sock?

A. A hook, line, and a stinker!

*

Q. What kind of music should you listen to when fishing?

A. Something catchy!

*

For a Great Fishermen Who Has Everything by Bruce Miller and Team Golfwell

Q. Why did Noah not do much fishing on the ark?

A. Because he had only two worms.

*

Q. What is the easiest way of catching a fish in one day?

A. Have someone throw it to you.

*

Q. What were the two magicians talking about while fishing?

A. One of them was asking the other one to pick a cod, any cod.

*

Q. Why are fishermen advised not to tell any jokes while going fishing on the ice?

A. It will crack them up!

*

Q. What would you call a fish wearing a tie?

A. So-fish-ticated.

*

For a Great Fishermen Who Has Everything by Bruce Miller and Team Golfwell

Q. What happened when the scientist crossed a fish and an elephant together?

A. Swimming trunks.

*

Q. Do you know what the shark said after eating a clownfish?

A. It tasted a little bit funny!

*

Q. Why don't fish like playing basketball?

A. Because fish are afraid of the net!

*

Q. Why don't oysters like to share their pearls?

A. Because they're shellfish!

*

Q. Who loves to eat at underwater restaurants?

A. Scuba diners.

*

Q. Have you ever wondered why oysters love going to the gym?

For a Great Fishermen Who Has Everything by Bruce Miller and Team Golfwell

A. It's good for their mussels.

*

Q. Did you hear about the new automobile that runs on seafood?

A. It is very e-fish-ent.

*

Q. Why does the blind man have a hard time eating fish?

A. He can't seafood.

*

Q. What do sea monsters usually eat?

A. They eat fish and ships.

*

Q. Where does a killer whale go for braces?

A. The 'ORCA-dontist.

*

Q. Why do some fish live at the bottom of the ocean?

A. Because they dropped out of school.

For a Great Fishermen Who Has Everything by Bruce Miller and Team Golfwell

*

Q. What did the aquarium manager say when his staff finally found the dwarf minnow hiding in one of their massive tanks?

A. Long time no sea.

*

Q. Why will the fish never take responsibility?

A. Because it's always salmon else's fault.

*

If you know of any better puns. Let minnow.

The rutabaga and banana. A rutabaga and a banana are in a boat. The rutabaga became bored with the boat ride, so the rutabaga started rocking the boat.

The banana got annoyed and told the rutabaga to stop. So, the rutabaga stopped rocking.

A few minutes later, the rutabaga again became bored and began rocking the boat. The banana became angry and told the rutabaga to stop rocking the boat. So, the rutabaga stopped.

Ten minutes later, the rutabaga laughed at the banana and said, "Hey this is fun!" And again, the rutabaga started rocking the boat.

The banana got angry and said, "Hey! Don't rock this stinkin' boat or I'm going to throw your butt out of this boat!"

The rutabaga stopped.

Ten minutes later, the rutabaga was at it again and the banana pushed the rutabaga off the boat!

Last joke not funny? Here's another. The ring. A young man was in love and proposed to his girlfriend and gave her a beautiful engagement ring right before he went into the army.

After he was discharged from the army, his future bride told him her mother had since become an invalid who needed her for round-the-clock care - 24/7. She told him she still loved him very much but didn't want to ruin his life.

Sadly, he told her to keep the ring and he understood her situation, but they decided once a year to meet at a nearby lake on the dock where he first proposed to her.

So, every year they met on the dock until as the years passed, the man developed Alzheimer's and went to the wrong dock for their annual meeting. He waited and waited and decided to fish while he was waiting.

Meanwhile, his beloved girlfriend is on the right dock but after waiting and waiting, she gave up and tossed the engagement ring into the lake thinking he did not love her anymore and left.

The old gentleman was still fishing on the wrong dock but suddenly felt a tug on his line. He reeled it in slowly and to his amazement, he caught…a rutabaga.

Stiff. A boy and his grandpa are out searching for nightcrawlers in their backyard to go fishing the next morning. The boy pulls out a huge nightcrawler and says, "Grandpa, look at this ONE!"

Grandpa says, "That's a big one you got there. Hey, bet ya 5 bucks you can't get that nightcrawler back in its hole."

The little boy says "Deal!" Then the little boy runs inside the house and into his grandparents' bathroom, lays the nightcrawler on the countertop, and grabs his grandma's hairspray and hairdryer. He sprays the worm with hairspray and dries it with the dryer. Pretty soon the nightcrawler is stiff and rigid.

The boy runs back outside to his grandpa and shows him his handy work. "Watch Grandpa." He sticks the nightcrawler back in its hole and then pulls it back out then throws it into the bucket with the other worms.

"Hey that's pretty smart, how'd you do that?" and the boy explained how he did it.

"That's pretty goods, well a bet is a bet. Here's your 5 bucks. I think we have enough worms to go fishing tomorrow. Let's head back into the house."

So, they go back into the house and the boy goes to bed. The next morning, the little boy wakes up excited to go fishing with his grandpa. He runs downstairs and sees his grandpa sitting at the table eating breakfast. The boy spots another 5 bucks on his placemat and says, "Grandpa, you already paid me for last night. What's this for?"

"Oh," says the grandpa pointing to the 5 dollars, "That's from your grandma."

Water is the most essential thing on earth. Without it, there would be no fishing.

-- Anon.

Skishing. The word "skishing" is a combination word from water skiing and fishing. It is like saltwater shore fishing but much more extreme. You wear a buoyant wetsuit and swim out from shore with flippers to fish with a rod and reel such as a surfcasting rod. Often live eels are used for bait. "It is practiced as a means of getting further out to sea to increase the chances of catching a fish and can be dangerous. The term skishing is a portmanteau of water-skiing and fishing because when hooked the stripers pull the angler through the water." [28]

Note that you get pulled along by the fish while you fight it. A large fish might drag you hundreds of yards by the time you reel it in. It is annoying to fishermen on the shore. [29]

Money cannot buy happiness, but it can buy fishing gear and that's pretty much the same thing.

Just an ordinary commoner. The most common fish in the oceans of the world of any of the species is the "Argyripnus" sometimes called a "bristle mouth." The fish is about the size of a small minnow. It is caught at 500 meters or deeper all over the world. [30]

Argyripnus is an oceanic ray-finned fish genus in the marine hatchet fish family.

Argyripnus or Bristle mouth

Fishing docks. "Look at where Jesus went to pick people. He didn't go to the colleges; he got guys off the fishing docks."

    -- Jeff Foxworthy

Three things to tell the wife you are going fishing.

1. "I love you like a fish loves water."

2. "You are the only fish in the sea for me."

3. If those two don't work paste this line on the refrigerator, "One fine fisherman lives here, with the catch of his life."

Excuses when you don't catch fish.
- The water was too cold.
- The water was too hot.
- I was trophy hunting.
- They were just touchy today. A few flashes and fins.
- It was all fished out.
- The water was too high.
- The water was too low.
- My hooks weren't sharp enough.
- It was raining.
- It was too sunny.
- I was working on my technique.
- The Solunar calendar predicted this. I know the Solunar theory is a hypothesis that fish move according to the location of the moon in comparison to their bodies, but I spilled coffee on the calendar and couldn't read it.
- It was too windy.
- It wasn't windy enough.
- The fish hit while I was in the john.
- Trolling too fast.
- Trolling too slow.

- The barometer was rising.
- The barometer was falling.
- The fish were facing the wrong way.
- Fish fear me.
- I forgot to take off the hook protector.
- I forgot the bait.
- I forgot my tackle.
- I forgot the beer.

Large lettering on the back of your favorite fishing vest:

IF YOU CAN READ THIS

YOU NEED TO FIND

YOUR OWN SPOT.

Angler. "An angler is a man who spends rainy days sitting on a muddy bank of rivers doing nothing because his wife won't let him do it at home."

Worry. "My biggest worry is that my wife will try to sell my fishing gear for what I said I paid for it."

For a Great Fishermen Who Has Everything by Bruce Miller and Team Golfwell

Teach fishing. "Sell a man a fish, he eats for a day, teach a man how to fish, you ruin a wonderful business opportunity."

"Give a man a fish, and he has food for a day. Teach him how to fish and you can get rid of him for the entire weekend!"

    -- Anon.

Fishing poem

Wind from the West

Fish bite the best.

Wind from the East

Fish bite the least.

Wind from the North

Do not go forth.

Wind from the South

Blows bait in their mouth.

An old one. A woman wanted to go ice fishing. So, she read several books on the subject, and finally, after getting all the necessary equipment together, she made her way out onto the ice.

After positioning her comfy stool, she started to make a circular cut in the ice.

Frighteningly, from up above, a voice boomed, 'There are no fish under the ice.'

Startled, the woman moved farther down the ice, poured herself a large coffee, and began to cut yet another hole.

Again, from the heavens, the voice bellowed, 'There are no fish under the ice.'

The lady, now became very concerned so she moved way down to the opposite end of the ice, set up her stool, and began again to cut her ice-hole.

The voice rang out once more, 'There are no fish under the ice.'

The lady stopped, looked upwards, and said, 'Is that you, Lord?'

The voice replied, 'No, this is the Ice-Rink Manager.'

Double win. "Fishing adds years to your life, and life to your years."

--Anon.

Did you know? Lungfish can live out of water for several years. They secrete mucus and build a cocoon and burrow under the earth. It takes in air with its lung through a built-in breathing tube that leads to the surface. A lungfish has both gills and a lung. [31]

The oldest known age for a lungfish was an Australian lungfish. In 2003, it was still alive and well at 65 years old. [32]

Sunday school. One recent Sunday, a young boy arrived at his Sunday school class late.

His teacher knew that the boy was usually very prompt and asked him if anything was wrong.

The boy replied nothing was wrong and he was going to go fishing, but his dad told him that he needed to go to church instead.

The teacher was very impressed and asked the boy if his father had explained to him why it was more important to go to church rather than to go fishing.

"Yes, ma'am, he did. My dad said that he didn't have enough bait for both of us."

Respecting privacy. "There are only two occasions when Americans respect privacy, especially in Presidents. Those are prayer and fishing."

　　-- Herbert Hoover

Skarping. It is a bit insane and hilarious to watch. Skarping is a highly unusual way to catch fish that began near Peoria Illinois where Asian carp were numerous and these carp literally jump out of the water when a boat passes. The boater pulls a skier and a basketball hoop behind the boat and motors through the waterway and when the carp jump, the skier catches the carp jumping out of the water with a hand net and drops it through the basketball net into a container.

Skarping is exciting to watch and there are You Tubes [33] (see the link referenced at 33 at the end of this book) and you can search YouTube by just searching the word, "Skarping."

Crazy Baits. Did you know chunks of soap with no added scents or chemicals, and homemade lye soaps can be used for catching catfish? Fishermen have been using them for hundreds of years. [34]

One Southern US fisherman used canned meat and broke the World Record at that time for catching the largest catfish ever caught with a rod and reel by reeling in a 116-pound, 12-ounce blue catfish.

Dogfood wrapped in cheesecloth can be used to catch carp, catfish, and panfish.

Chicken livers due to their smell can be used for catfish as well as freshwater bass.

Raisins, mulberries, and persimmons. Carp have been known to congregate in lakes in areas with overhanging berry bushes.

Trout have been known to go for the sweet smell of freshly chewed bubble gum.

Candy, gummy worms, etc. have a sweetness that some say attracts fish as well.

Trout, bluegill, sunfish, etc. have been caught on mini marshmallows.

Spoiled bacon has a strong smell that is attractive to fish and bacon fat has oils that attract bluegills, crappies, and catfish.

Peanut butter sandwiches have been known to attract codfish, catfish, carp, and bluegills.

Bottle caps curled to look like a lure with a hook attached, shoelaces, zucchini, cucumber, spam, pom-poms have also been used as baits. [35]

I only fish on days that end in 'Y'.

Girls who like fishing are gifts from God and deserve bigger diamonds.

Braggart: "Last week at this spot the pH factor was just right, and I caught fifteen 7-pounders right here."

"Yeah, right," his buddy said, "I don't know about the pH factor, but the BS factor here is going through the roof."

Pacific Hagfish can secrete a bucket of slime in less than a minute. They can be found at deep depths such as about 300 meters off the Northwest US Pacific Coast. The slime is a defense mechanism to confuse predators. [36]

Hard work and luck. "Fishing is quite a good metaphor for life. You do your prep, you do your thinking, you put your bait out, and you wait, confident that you've done your groundwork. But a lot of life is luck."

    -- Jeremy Wade

Women puzzle over this. How does my husband sit on the dock and stare at a bobber for an hour but is totally impatient to wait five minutes to let me finish putting my makeup on?

Speedy sailfish. Did you know that the fastest swimming fish in the ocean is the sailfish? Sailfish can swim over 65 mph (105 kph).

Some of the most popular places for catching sailfish are off the west coast of Costa Rica, or Panama. The Florida Keys, Isla Mujeres, Mexico, the Pacific Coast off Panama, Mozambique, Exmouth, Australia, and a few others are also considered excellent for sailfish.

Finding new places. "There are always new places to go fishing. For any fisherman, there's always a new place, always a new horizon.

For a Great Fishermen Who Has Everything by Bruce Miller and Team Golfwell

-- Jack Nicklaus

The right bait. An old one. Two fully equipped fishermen went fishing with all the best equipment money could buy with the latest in poles, reels, etc.

After two hours they caught nothing.

Then arrives next to them a 10-year-old kid with a long tree branch, string, and a crooked pin and begins to catch one fish after another. He has a stringer full of very nice fish when one of the two men asks him how in the world does he catch so many fish?

The kid says "Hmm hmm hmm hmm hmm hmm hmm… "

"What did you say?"

"hmm hmm hmm hmm hmm hmm hmm hmm "

"WHAT?"

Then the kid spits out a few worms in his hand. "You have to keep the worms warm!"

Convincing the wife. "I've managed to convince my wife that somewhere in the Bible it says, 'Man cannot have too many shotguns and fishing poles.'"

For a Great Fishermen Who Has Everything by Bruce Miller and Team Golfwell

-- Norman Schwarzkopf

Lesson in History The king wanted to go fishing and he asked the royal weather forecaster the forecast for the next few hours. The palace meteorologist assured him that there was no chance of rain.

So, the king and the queen went fishing. On the way, they met a man with a fishing pole riding on a donkey, and the king asked the man if the fish were biting.

The fisherman said, "Your Majesty, you should return to the palace! In just a short time I expect a huge rainstorm."

The king replied: "I hold the palace meteorologist in high regard. He is an educated and experienced professional. Besides, I pay him very high wages. He gave me a very different forecast. I trust him."

So, the king continued on his way. However, in a short time, torrential rain fell from the sky. The King and Queen were totally soaked.

Furious, the king returned to the palace and gave the order to fire the meteorologist. Then he summoned the fisherman and offered him the prestigious position of royal forecaster.

The fisherman said, "Your Majesty, I do not know anything about forecasting. I obtain my information from my donkey. If I see my donkey's ears drooping, it means with certainty that it will rain."

So, the king hired the donkey.

And thus began the practice of hiring dumb asses to work in influential positions of forecasting weather.

Fly rod. Man: Can I have a fly rod and reel for my son?

Fishing Shop Owner: Sorry sir we don't do trades.

A fishing fable for kids or grandkids. In a huge pond, there lived a lot of fish. They were arrogant and never listened to anyone. In this pond, there also lived a kind-hearted crocodile.

He advised the fish, "It does not pay to be arrogant and overconfident. It could be your downfall."

But the fish never listened to him. "There's that crocodile advising us again," they would say.

One afternoon, the crocodile was resting beside a stone near the pond, when two fishermen stopped there to drink water.

The fishermen noticed that the pond had many fish. "Look! This pond is full of fish. Let's come here tomorrow with our fishing net," said one of them.

"I'm surprised we haven't seen this place before!" exclaimed the other.

The crocodile heard all this. When the fishermen left, he slowly slipped into the pond and went straight to the fish. "You all had better leave this pond before dawn. Early morning those two fishermen are going to come to this pond with their net," warned the crocodile.

But the fish just laughed and said, "There have been many fishermen who have tried to catch us. These two are not going to catch us either. Don't you worry about us, Mr. Crocodile," they said mockingly.

The next morning, the fishermen came and threw their net in the pond. The nets were big and strong. Very soon all the fish were caught.

"If only we had listened to Mr. Crocodile. He only wanted to help us. For our arrogance we must pay with our lives," said the fish as they were hauled out of the water.

The fishermen took the foolish fish to the market and sold them for a good profit.

Finding peace. "I don't go fishing to find myself, but to lose myself."

    -- Anon.

Fishing guides. "Like they say, you can learn more from a guide in one day than you can in three months fishing alone."

    -- Mario Lopez

Fishing trip. A woman meets with her lover, who is also her husband's best friend. They make love for hours. Afterward, as they lie in bed, the phone rings. Since it's the woman's house, she picks up the receiver.

The best friend listens, only hearing her side of the conversation, "Hello? Oh, hi... I'm so glad that you called... Really? That's wonderful... Well, I'm happy to hear you're having such a great time... Oh, that sounds terrific... Love you, too. OK. Bye-bye."

She hangs up the telephone and her lover asks, "Who was that?"

"Oh," she replies, "That was my husband telling me about the wonderful time he's having on his fishing trip with you."

A delusion. Fishing is a delusion all surrounded by liars in old clothes.

-- Don Marquis

Pants on fire. Before the start of the fishing season, an angler who hadn't gotten a fishing license was casting away trying to catch some trout in a local stream. A stranger slowly approaches and asks, "Any luck?"

"Any luck? Heck yes, this is a wonderful spot. I took 10 out of this stream yesterday," he boasted.

"Is that so? By the way, do you know who I am?" asks the stranger.

"Nope."

"Well, I'm the new game warden."

"Oh," gulped the fisherman... "Well, do you know who I am?"

"Nope," said the game warden.

"Meet the biggest liar in the state."

A simple and wonderful woman. "My grandmother was a very simple woman. She didn't want a whole lot. My grandmother wanted to go to church and Sunday school every Sunday. She wanted to be in Bible study every Wednesday. The other days, she wanted to be on a fishing creek."

--Shannon Sharpe, Former NFL player, and sports commentator.

Thanks, dad. "My dad taught me how to fish. When I am stand in a trout stream now, and I have the waders on, and I've got a fly rod in my hand, or I am fishing for bass, I think of sitting in a boat with my dad. How can that be a bad experience?"

-- Matt Lauer

No fisherman? "Without the fisherman, there is no fish."

For a Great Fishermen Who Has Everything by Bruce Miller and Team Golfwell

— Lailah Gifty Akita, Author

Surprise rescue. Standing at the edge of the lake, a man saw a woman flailing about in the deep water.

Unable to swim, the man screamed for help and a nearby fisherman ran up.

The man said, "My wife is drowning, and I can't swim! Please save her! I'll give you a hundred dollars!"

The fisherman immediately dove into the water…

In ten powerful strokes, he reached the woman, put his arm around her, and swam back to shore.

Depositing her at the feet of the man, the fisherman said, "Okay, where's my hundred dollars?"

The man said, "Look, when I saw her going down for the third time, I thought it was my wife. But this is my mother-in-law."

The fisherman reaches into his pocket and says, "Just my luck. How much do I owe you?"

For a Great Fishermen Who Has Everything by Bruce Miller and Team Golfwell

Give a man a fish and he'll eat for a day. Teach a man to fish and,
- He will buy graphite rods
- Reels
- Spinnerbaits
- Jigs
- Crankbaits
- Jerk baits
- Plastics
- Flies
- Waders
- A boat
- And a truck.

Addicted. "I grew up in Florida and started fishing with my dad going down to the Everglades and around the state, plus some offshore stuff for sails and wahoo - but I never really got the bug until my husband, and I went float fishing on the Snake River at Jackson Hole for trout. I've been pretty much addicted ever since."

-- Shannon Bream, Journalist for Fox News

Racoon swordfish story. "Fishing for swordfish can be difficult as they typically weigh from 100 pounds to approximately 400 pounds.

Experience and heavy gear are necessary. Swordfish are night feeders so it's best to go out miles until you're in waters between 75 and 300 feet deep.

This night it was rough with seas between three to five feet, so the boat was rolling while we waited for a hit. Suddenly something crawled out from the bottom of the boat compartment. It was a raccoon, and the raccoon was acting crazy and made us think it had rabies, so we went up top and let the raccoon have the run of the boat.

Eventually, after twenty minutes or so, we guessed that the raccoon was in fact only seasick. Finally, the raccoon crawled back into the bilge and stayed there for the remainder of our trip.

We continued fishing and did catch a swordfish and returned home with it and the unwelcomed seasick raccoon still on board. Sometime that night, the raccoon crawled out of the bilge and didn't set foot on the boat again. We figured it must have learned its lesson."

-- Anon.

African Remora fishing. In some parts of Africa, the natives use Remora suckerfish catch larger fish. They tie a line to a Remora and release it to find a host. After allowing time for the fish to attach itself, which is indicated when the line goes tight, the Remora and the fish it is attached to are pulled into the boat. Then the Remora is used again to fish and so on.

When in Rome... Two Florida anglers were way up north and went out to try ice fishing for the first time. They'd been at it for hours and hadn't caught a thing.

"I don't know what we're doing wrong," said the first man.

Just then, a local passed on a snowmobile with a whole bucket of fish on the back.

The second said, "That's why we're not catching anything, we're not trolling!"

Unwelcome surprise. A man comes home from a two-week fishing trip and learns his teenage daughter is pregnant. Angry, he begins throwing things around in the house then sits down with a bottle of whiskey and starts to drink away his sorrow. "What's his name?" he asks his daughter.

"He's coming over to meet you dad, but please don't make a scene. Yes, he's married. I'm sorry."

The father struggles to control his rage when a red Ferrari pulls up in front of the house and a handsome, very well-dressed, and somewhat familiar-looking man gets out. He walks up the stairs and into the house.

Before anyone can say anything, the handsome man says, "Yes, I'm a very famous person, I have a family, and I cannot leave them. However, I will take care of your daughter as well. If your daughter gives birth to a boy, he will inherit two of my manufacturing plants, plus $20 million, and he will get a fine education at the best university I can afford. Your daughter will also have lifetime support of $2 million a year.

"If she gives birth to a girl, the baby will inherit one of my factories, plus $10 million, and she will get an education in the best university I can afford, and your daughter will have a lifetime support of $1 million."

"What if I have a miscarriage?" the daughter asks.

The father stands up and puts another glass on the table, pours the man a drink and puts his hand on his shoulder, and says, "Then you will try again ..."

Good question. Two young salmon are swimming along one day. As they do, they are passed by a wiser, older fish coming the other way.

The wiser fish greets the two young ones as he passes, saying, "Morning boys, how's the water?"

The other two continue to swim in silence for a little while until the first one turns to the other and asks, "What the heck is water?"

For a Great Fishermen Who Has Everything by Bruce Miller and Team Golfwell

Taste. Smoked carp tastes just as good as smoked salmon when you ain't got no smoked salmon.

    -- Patrick F. McManus, Humorist and columnist for Outdoor Life, Field & Stream.

Phone in the lake. "My oldest brother lost his phone for the fifth time in a lake. I have been texting to his phone all the fish jokes I can find. I am doing this since I suspect when his phone is replaced, he is going to be spammed with a ton of people jokes."

    -- Anon.

Therapy. Fishing is my therapy. It's such a great immersion into life.

    --Robson Green, English actor, angler, singer-songwriter and presenter, *Extreme Fishing*.

Q. What's the difference between a hypochondriac and a fishing fanatic?

A. Nothing. Neither of them must catch anything to indulge their obsession.

Outdoors. Raise your kids near the water with a fishing pole. So, they won't be hanging around the house with a gaming console.

For a Great Fishermen Who Has Everything by Bruce Miller and Team Golfwell

-- Anon.

An old one you might have heard. After a Tuesday fishing on the River Test, near Southampton in Southern England, Trevor is walking from the pier carrying two brown trout in a bucket.

He is approached by a Water Conservation Officer who asks him for his fishing license.

Trevor replies to the environmentalist, "I was not fishing, and I did not catch these brown trout, they are my pets. Every day I come down to the water and put these fish into the water and take them for a walk to the end of the pier and back. When I'm ready to go I whistle, and they jump back into the bucket, and we go home."

The officer does not believe him, and he reminds Trevor that it is illegal to fish without a license. The fisherman turns to the warden and says, "If you don't believe me then watch," and he throws the trout back into the water.

The warden says, "Now whistle to your fish and show me that they will jump out of the water and into the bucket."

Trevor turns to the officer and says, "What fish?"

Time for fishing. "Hell, if I'd jumped on all the dames I'm supposed to have jumped on, I'd have had no time to go fishing."

-- Clark Gable

Needs a second opinion. An offshore fisherman got caught in a huge storm and his large fishing boat was sinking. He kept trying to battle the huge waves, but they were constantly coming over the bow filling his vessel. He prayed out loud. "Help! Is there anybody up there?" he shouted.

A majestic voice boomed through the dark clouds, "I will help you, my son, but first you must have faith in me."

"Yes, yes, I trust you!" cried the fisherman.

"Let go of the wheel," boomed the voice.

There was a long pause, and the man shouted up again, "But that will sink the boat completely if I don't keep the bow into these waves!"

"Let go of the wheel," boomed the voice again.

"Is there anybody ELSE up there?"

Ocean City Maryland and Cabo San Lucas here I come! The White Marlin Open is considered by many as the biggest and richest bill fishing tournament in the world. It has been held annually for 48 years giving out over 86 million in prize money.

"The first tournament was held in 1974 and drew 57 boats, 150 anglers, and paid $20,000 in prize money. The 2021 event drew 444 boats, over 3,500 contestants, and awarded over $9.2 million dollars in prize money, including the top individual prize of $3.2 million dollars which established a new world record award for the catch of a fish!" [37]

There is another very well-known tournament in Cabo San Lucas, Mexico, called the Bisbee Black and Blue Marlin Tournament which also is one of the largest tournaments in the world and has millions of dollars in prizes. [38] During tournament week many anglers report that Cabo turns into one giant party, so you don't have to be on a boat to have some fun.

The memory of a fish. Many believe fish have memories and can be trained to recognize different colors and remember them. We understand a retired professor claims to have done research showing if the fish is given food only when one light (say red) burns and then not given the food when the other light (say white, green, or yellow) is on over 15 to 20 days, the fish memorize this and come to the spot of feeding only if the red light burns. Many other studies have been done to show fish recognize color. [39]

"It is popularly believed that fish have a memory span of only 30 seconds. Canadian scientists, however, have demonstrated that this is far from true -- in fact, fish can remember context and associations up to twelve days later." [40]

Thinking and fishing. "I do fish. I think there is a connection between thinking and fishing mostly because you spend a lot of time up to your waist in water without a whole lot to keep your mind busy."

-- Anthony Doerr, Pulitzer Prize winning author.

Not perfect. "I'm not perfect and I know it. I've done all sorts of things that are frowned upon these days - big-game hunting, fishing. I still enjoy fishing, but I don't kill warm-blooded animals anymore - I make an exception with birds sometimes."

-- Wilbur Smith

From birth to death anyone can fish. I just think it's fantastic to see old people going fishing with young people and teaching them things.

-- Rex Hunt, Australian TV personality

All kinds of fishing tournaments. [41] Fishing tournaments come in all shapes and sizes such as the Midwest Open Ice Fishing Tournament in Wampler's Lake in Brooklyn, Michigan, for the annual two-person ice fishing team event, and only one line is allowed in the water at a time, and you can choose to fish with or without a shelter.

Over the past 20 years in Eddyville, Kentucky, there is the Muzzy Classic for bow fishermen from all over the country. They usually have 100 boats to take to Kentucky lakes and the Tennessee and Cumberland rivers, to show off the unique mix of archery, hunting, fishing, and bravado that comprises bowfishing.

The no fishing pole necessary Redneck Fishing Tournament in downstate Bath, Illinois. Competitors wearing colorful costumes use nets to catch Asian carp from the Illinois River—the boat motors cause the fish to jump skyward. Winning boats have caught hundreds of fish in just a few hours. The carp are a safety risk in warmer months, so since 2006, the Redneck Fishing Tournament has served to decrease their numbers and raise money for veterans in need. [42]

Mountain Music Kids Fishing Tournament is for those 16 and under and held in Douglas Lake in Sevierville, Tennessee, for the past 30 years. Every child who participates receives an award and a photo with their catch and the top 100 catches get cash prizes. [43]

Born to sell. A young man from Texas moves to California and goes to a big department store looking for a job. The manager says, "Do you have any sales experience?"

The young man says, "Yeah, I was a salesman back home in Texas."

Well, the boss liked the young guy, so he gave him the job. "You start tomorrow. I'll come down after we close and see how you did."

His first day on the job was rough but he got through it. After the store hours, the boss came down. "How many sales did you make today?"

The young man says, "One."

For a Great Fishermen Who Has Everything by Bruce Miller and Team Golfwell

"Just one? Our salespeople average 20 or 30 sales a day. How much was the sale for?"

The young man says, "$101,237.64."

The boss raises his eyebrows and says, "$101,237.64?! What the hell did you sell him?"

"First I sold him a small fishhook. Then I sold him a medium fishhook. Then I sold him a larger fishhook. Then I sold him a new fishing rod. Then I asked him where he was going fishing, and he said down at the coast, so I told him he was gonna need a boat, so we went down to the boat department, and I sold him that twin engine Chris Craft."

"Wow!" The boss says.

"Then he said he didn't think his Honda Civic would pull it, so I took him down to the automotive department and sold him that 4X4 Blazer."

"So, you're telling me a guy came in here to buy a fishhook and you sold him a boat and truck?"

The young man says, "No, he came in here to buy a box of tampons for his wife, and I said, 'Well, since your weekend's shot, you might as well go fishing.'"

The one that got away. Maybe many of you have experienced something like this? It was reported by an avid Florida fisherman who couldn't say how big it was, but whatever it was, it pulled a 25' Sea Ray boat, 1/4 mile up the Intercoastal Waterway, against the current. He reported,

For a Great Fishermen Who Has Everything by Bruce Miller and Team Golfwell

"I had gone fishing in the Intercoastal Waterway, outside Fort Lauderdale, Florida. I was catching nothing. Finally, I decided to check my bait. As soon as I did, it seemed I was hung. I slammed the rod up down, right, and left with no results. Then my friend who was fishing with me did the same. Nothing. He handed me the rod back and said, 'You're going to have to cut it off.'

Just about then my line extended out at a forty-five-degree angle and began moving up current! I tried to turn whatever it was but that clearly wasn't going to happen. Soon we realized that the entire boat was moving steadily up current, despite also being anchored. It kept going to my shock and continued pulling the boat for about 15 minutes.

Then it stopped in a deep hole, and nothing could entice it to engage further. I jerked and jerked. Then implored my friend to try to make it re-engage by dropping the anchor on it. But he ignored me. He insisted on taking a turn at jerking on the rod which I did not want but had no choice as it was his rod and boat.

The moment that he jerked the first jerk, he was thrown back by the recoil of his pull. The large hook had broken in half. There are only three things I can think of that can do what that fish did. A huge Ray, a giant Goliath Grouper, or a big Shark.

The Ray or the Goliath Grouper are the best candidates as they are both happy to hug the bottom."

    -- Anon.

Sounds. Fish use a variety of low-pitched sounds to convey messages to each other. They moan, grunt, croak, boom, hiss, whistle, creak, shriek, and wail. They rattle their bones and gnash their teeth. However, fish do not have vocal cords. They use other parts of their bodies to make noises, such as vibrating muscles against their swim bladder. [44]

Love to fish. "I like fishing. Not actual fishing - I like the peace and quiet of being at sea. It's different."

-- Rafael Nadal

Indecent. "I've spent as much of my life fishing as decency allowed, and sometimes I don't let even that get in my way."

-- Thomas McGuane, Author.

Another big fish story. "While working on an Alaskan salmon boat that started in Bellingham, Washington and ending in Dutch Harbor, Alaska, and about 60 days into the season, we decided to fish for halibut. If you have ever fished for halibut, you get the joke. Honestly, it's the most boring fishing on the planet. We took seine netting twine, tied a big hook on one end, lowered it to the bottom of the harbor with a big chunk of lovely, fresh salmon on it as bait. Tied it off to the railing of the boat and sat down to drink and talk.

Every 30 minutes, we'd walk around and check out the long lines by tugging on the line and seeing if it was heavy. I tugged and felt nothing, then a 10 lb. halibut was on the next

For a Great Fishermen Who Has Everything by Bruce Miller and Team Golfwell

line. We pulled it up, hand over hand, and talked about how it should be cooked for dinner. Then I pulled on the next line. It didn't move. I yelled to the first mate and the deckhand to bring me a knife, as I thought I was stuck on a rock.

Others came over and tugged at it, trying to save our hook from being lost. It moved a little. They tugged harder. I came and tugged too. And then it tugged back. Hard. I mean really hard. So hard that the netting twine slid through my hands and burned my palms, drawing blood. Then a sharp downward tug trapped my hand under the rope against the ship!

I was crying out in alarm and others came over to free me. We all tugged and pulled, but no way were we going to get this thing up where we could see it, so we wheeled the winch out, hooked the twine to it, and pulled up a 185-pound halibut! Dinner and a show!"

-- Anon.

Expensive. "Women are like fish; fun to catch, fresh ones are better and when you decide to keep one, it will cost you a lot of money."

-- Anon.

On tour, I'll get up at 5 p.m. and go to bed at 8 in the morning. With fishing, it's the exact opposite. Fishing is the only healthy thing I do. Touring is such a grind; it's the opposite of healthy.

-- Dean Ween, Guitarist, singer, songwriter

From a woman's perspective. "A man's 'one last cast' is like a woman's 'I'll be ready in 5 minutes!'"

"Women know why men love to go fishing. It is the only time they will hear the words 'Wow, that's a big one!'"

"A real woman will not make you choose between her and fishing, she will make you take her fishing."

"Only Average girls dance on poles, the best ones fish with them."

    -- Anon.

Catching a fish with a snake. There is an unusual video on YouTube [45] where one fisherman caught a fish using a live snake on his line to bite the fish, snagging it with its teeth, and he reeled up the snake with the fish attached. The fisherman appears to use the snake to prey on fish and used a spoon lure to hook the snake on its side and then lowered it into the water. [46]

Getting off the couch. "The world needs more tackle boxes and fewer Xboxes."

    -- Anon.

Thanks wife! "I used to play football, and then my wife bought me a fishing rod."

For a Great Fishermen Who Has Everything by Bruce Miller and Team Golfwell

-- John Rocha

The largest fish ever caught. According to IGFA records, the largest fish ever caught was a great white shark that weighed an unbelievable 2,664 pounds (1,208.389 kg.). Caught off the coast of Ceduna, Australia, in 1959, it took angler Alfred Dean just 50 minutes to win the fight against this one-ton shark. That's an amazing feat when you're reeling in the largest shark ever caught! [47]

There is a picture of it on Instagram. [48] Out of the 30 sportfishing world-records on this list, 11 of them weighed in at more than 1,000 pounds, but this great white shark was the only fish to weigh in at more than 2,000 pounds. With almost 900 pounds separating this catch from the second-place tiger shark, Dean should easily continue to hold his world record for the largest fish ever caught for at least another 60 years. [49]

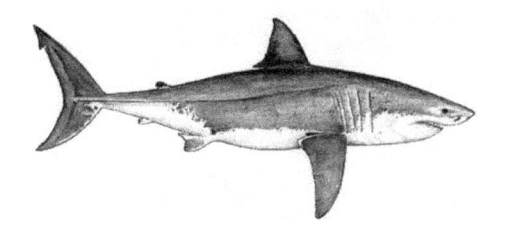

All-Star game v. Fishing. "The only thing bad about winning the pennant is that you have to manage the All-Star Game the next year. I'd rather go fishing for three days."

-- Whitey Herzog

Did you know fish help each other? According to the SPCA species of fish work together to hunt prey. "Fish, such as groupers and coral trout, will send a visual signal to show other fish the location of a hidden prey. Together, they will catch prey at a higher rate than when hunting alone." [50]

Simple. "I wondered how simple we really are. That we can do the same things again and again and again and find them interesting, even fascinating and seek the repetition with a hunger as avid. How fishing was like that, and painting."

— Peter Heller, The Painter

Refreshments. "Fishing, with me, has always been an excuse to drink in the daytime."

-- Jimmy Cannon, Sports journalist

IGFA World Records. The IGFA has a site that has all world records for fish and the link to the site is referenced here. [51] The IGFA site also shows you how to submit a fish for a record as well. [52]

Confusion sometimes arises over the blue whale being the largest fish on the planet but as you probably know the blue whale is a mammal and not a fish.

Acting. "It's a little like casting out hundreds of fishing lines into the audience. You start getting little bites, then more, then you hook a few, then more. Then you can start reeling them in and that's a loveliest feeling - the whole audience laughing with you."

-- Jim Dale, Actor, composer, director, and songwriter.

Relief. "The fishing is a great relief for me. When I'm out there's no cell phone ringing. I'm out there fishing with bears. I'm in the middle of God's country catching tons of fish. I just absolutely love it."

-- Rick Barry, NBA retired.

Charter captain and the IRS. The IRS suspected a fishing boat owner wasn't paying proper wages to his Deckhand, so they sent an agent to investigate him.

IRS Agent: "I need a list of your employees and how much you pay them."

Boat Owner: "Well, there's Clarence, my deckhand, he's been with me for 3 years. I pay him $1,000 a week plus free room and board. Then there's the mentally challenged guy. He works about 18 hours every day and does about 90% of the work around here. He makes about $30 per week, pays his own room and board, and I buy him a bottle of Bacardi rum and a dozen Budweiser's every Saturday night so he can cope with life. He also gets to sleep with my wife occasionally."

IRS Agent: "That's the guy I want to talk to - the mentally challenged one."

Boat Owner: "That would be me. What would you like to know?"

Don't bother me. "Don't bother me when I'm fishing unless you got beer."

-- Anon.

Alone with nature. "I like Alaska for the salmon fishing - it's fantastic there. I usually stay in a log cabin with no one around for miles. I like to go with friends, but I'm also happy to be on my own with nature."

-- Vinnie Jones

Love seafood. "Mobile is a seaport town, and we ate a lot of seafood. We'd go fishing, we'd catch our fish, and we'd eat our fish. It was a ritual on Saturday morning for all my family - my grandfather, my brothers, my uncles, my father - to go fishing, and then the ladies of the family would clean the fish and fry them up."

-- Billy Williams, Major League Baseball Hall of Fame. (Chicago Cubs)

The Pope. The Pope dies and stands in front of the gates of heaven. St. Peter looks at him confused. "Who are you? I don't know you."

The Pope says, "I'm the Pope, the Holy Father."

Peter scrolls through his holy book, "Pope, Pope, Holy Father.... nope, not in here,"

Now the Pope is confused "But I'm God's representative on earth."

St. Peter says, "Pease wait a minute" and rushes to God's office. Out of breath, he asks God, "Excuuuse me Boss, there is someone standing at the gates saying his name is Pope and he's your representative on earth."

God is puzzled and says, "What in hell? I have a what on earth? JEEEEESUS, come over here son!"

Jesus comes over, "Yes Dad, what's up?"

God asks him "Go to the gates and have a look at that guy saying he's, my representative."

Jesus heads off and returns a few minutes later, laughing out loud. "Dad, do you remember the small fishing club I founded about 2000 years ago?"

"Yes, I do," says God.

"You won't believe it, it still exists."

Want to go fishing? "Comedians get jokes offered to them, rock stars get women and underwear thrown onstage, and I get guys that want to take me fishing."

-- Les Claypool, Musician lead singer, bassist, primary songwriter, and only continuous member of the funk metal band Primus.

Smell the roses. "I look at trees, hunt mushrooms, and watch animals. Fishing is what gets me out into the woods so I can notice these things."

-- John D. Voelker

Fill it up. Three guys, one Irish, one English, and one Scottish are out walking along the beach together one day.

They come across a lantern and a Genie pops out of it. "I will give you each one wish, that's three wishes in total," says the Genie.

The Scottish guy says, "I am a fisherman, my dad's a fisherman, his dad was a fisherman, and my son will be one too. I want all the oceans full of fish for all eternity."

So, with a blink of the Genie's eye 'poof', the oceans were teaming with fish.

The Englishman was amazed, so he said, "I want a wall around England, protecting her, so that no one will get in for all eternity."

Again, with a blink of the Genie's eye 'poof' there was a huge wall around England.

The Irishman asks, "I'm very curious. Please tell me more about this wall."

The Genie explains, "Well, it's about 150 feet high, 50 feet thick, protecting England so that nothing can get in or out."

The Irishman says, "Fill it up with ocean water."

Like sex. "Fishing is like sex. When it is great it is great. When it is bad, it is still great!"

-- Anon.

Born to fish. I was born to fish. To get up early, fog on the water, sun rising and the world waking up. It realigns my soul with nature. It's who I am. It's my passion, my sanity, and my prayer.

-- Anon.

Old fisherman saying. It is better to sit in a boat and think about God than it is to sit in a church and think about fishing.

For a Great Fishermen Who Has Everything by Bruce Miller and Team Golfwell

Fishing for speeders. A man was speeding down an Alabama highway, feeling secure in a gaggle of cars all traveling at the same speed.

However, as they passed a speed trap, he got nailed with an infrared speed detector and was pulled over.

The officer handed him the citation, received his signature, and was about to walk away when the man asked, "Officer, I know I was speeding, but I don't think it's fair - there were plenty of other cars around me who were going just as fast, so why did I get the ticket?"

"Ever go a fishin'?" the policeman suddenly asked the man.

"Ummm, yeah..." the startled man replied.

The officer grinned and added, "Did you ever catch 'em all?"

All sizes. "Fish come in three sizes: small, medium, and the one that got away!"

-- Anon.

Knock-Knock.

Knock, knock.

Who's there?

For a Great Fishermen Who Has Everything by Bruce Miller and Team Golfwell

Fish.

Fish who?

Bless you!

*

Knock, knock.

Who's there?

Artie Fish.

Artie Fish who?

Artie Fish-el Intelligence.

A woman's view. "She laughed. 'I hope he will enjoy good sport – though my small experience informs me that catching fish is not necessary for your true angler's enjoyment.'

'Oh, no! But to lose a fish is quite another matter!'

'Certainly! One cannot wonder that it should cast even the most cheerful person into gloom, for it is always such an enormous one that escapes!'

'I begin to think you are yourself an angler, ma'am: you are so exactly right!'"

— Georgette Heyer, The Nonesuch

Fly fishermen. "Fly fishermen are born honest, but they get over it. And fly-fishing is the most fun you can have standing up."

    -- Anon.

Mark the spot. Joe and Moe rent a boat and go fishing. They catch a lot of fish and return to the shore. Bill says to Frank, "I hope you marked the spot where we caught all those fish."

Frank replies, "Yes, I marked an 'X' on the side of the boat to mark the spot."

Bill says to Frank sharply, "You idiot! How do you know we'll get the same boat?"

    -- Anon.

Beauty. "A poor fisherman who knows the beauties of the misty mornings is much richer than a wealthy man who sleeps till noon in his palace!"

    — Mehmet Murat ildan

Fish aren't dumb. Fish will avoid situations they know to cause them pain and will seek out things with rewards.

According to the SPCA, "Fish can also learn how to use tools. Many fish, for example, use rocks to crack open bivalves such as clams, oysters, and mussels for food.

"The archerfish specifically displays incredible intelligence. They learn how to catch prey items out of the air above them by shooting a stream of water at them, with the correct volume based on target size." [53] Fish have excellent schools!

Definition of a fish. "An animal that grows the fastest from the time it is caught to the time the fisherman describes it to his friends."

-- Anon.

Holy water. There is a priest, a rabbi, and an atheist are in a boat fishing in the middle of a lake. The priest says, "Oh heavens I forgot my lures." He gets out of the boat and walks across the water, gets his lures, and walks over the water back to the boat. The atheist is stunned.

The rabbi says, "Oh Yahweh, I forgot my bait. The rabbi gets out of the boat and walks across the water, gets his bait, and walks back to the boat. The atheist can't believe it.

The atheist still believing there is no God, says, "Oh I forgot my extra line." He gets out of the boat and makes a big splash and quickly sinks to the bottom.

The priest turns to the rabbi and says, "I guess we should have told him where the rocks were."

Three blondes are sitting by the side of a river holding fishing poles with the lines in the water.

A Game Warden comes up behind them, taps them on the shoulder, and says, "Excuse me, ladies, I'd like to see your fishing licenses."

"We don't have any," replied the first blonde.

"Well, if you're going to fish, you need fishing licenses," said the Game Warden.

"But officer," replied the second blonde, "we aren't fishing. We all have magnets at the end of our lines and we're collecting debris off the bottom of the river."

The Game Warden lifted all the lines and, sure enough, there were horseshoe magnets tied on the end of each line.

"Well, I know of no law against it," said the Game Warden. "Take all the debris you want."

And with that, he left.

As soon as the Game Warden was out of sight, the three blondes started laughing hysterically.

"What a dumb Fish Cop," the second blonde said to the other two. "Doesn't he know that there are steelhead trout in this river?"

Horseback Trawling. In Belgium, people trawl for shrimp on horseback following an old tradition that makes it easier to drag a shrimp net on the bottom. Horses are also used to drag other types of fishing nets to haul out their catch easier. Of course, using a boat is much more efficient, but this is still practiced in Europe today.

Once I retire and slow down, I don't want to be in New York. I want to be somewhere near a lake or a pond so that on my days when I have nothing to do, I can go fishing.

-- Sharon Jones, Singer, and entertainer.

How can you tell hold old a fish is? Scientists can figure out how old a fish is by counting growth rings on its scales The rings mark seasonal changes in fish growth, like the annual rings in tree trunks.

Scales have a series of fine rings that appear as the scale grows. In summer the rings are wider apart. In winter the rings are closer together because the fish grow more slowly. Each pair of rings indicates one year. [54]

Good things. "Good things come to those who BAIT."

-- Anon.

Negotiate. "A couple of months ago I went fishing with a buddy of mine, we pulled his boat into the dock, I lifted this big 'ol stringer of bass and this idiot on the dock goes, 'Hey, y'all catch all of them fish?'

'Nope - Talked 'em into giving up.'"

— Bill Engvall

For a Great Fishermen Who Has Everything by Bruce Miller and Team Golfwell

One thing. "There is only one thing that can keep me from fishing…

Never mind, just kidding!"

-- Anon.

It's the clothes. "I think it was really about the clothes. Nothing says real man like a vest with 38 pockets and a mesh hat with hooks in it."

— Craig Ferguson

Secret fishing spot. One angler says to another after not getting any bites for an hour, "How do you like my secret fishing spot?"

The other says, "Very nice, except…well I don't think the fish know about it either."

Priest catches a big fish. A priest was fishing in the country when he caught a really big fish. He hauled it up on the bank and this guy walked up and looked at it. He looked over at the priest and said, "Wow, that's a big son of a bitch!"

The priest looked over and said, "My son, I'm a man of the cloth. You shouldn't talk like that."

The guy looks at him and says, "That's what we call those fish in this part of the country."

The priest replied, "Oh, I see. I understand."

So, the priest takes the fish back to the rectory and a nun from the convent on church grounds walks up and says, "Wow, did you catch that on your fishing trip?"

The priest proudly holds the fish up and says, "Yes, I caught this son of a bitch!"

The nun looks at him and says, "Father!"

The priest says, "That's what they call these fish where I caught it!"

The nun says, "Would you like for me to clean that son of a bitch for you?"

The priest says, "That will be fine."

So, the nun is carrying it to clean it when another nun walks up and asks where she got it. The nun carrying the fish replies, "The father caught this son of a bitch!"

The nun that asked says, "Sister!"

The nun carrying the fish says, "That's what the father said they're called!"

The other nun says, "I'll bake that son of a bitch after you clean it then!"

Well, low and behold the Pope shows up for dinner. Everyone finishes dinner and the pope is sitting there, and he looks around, leans back, and says, "That was a fine meal you cooked for the Pontiff."

Well, the priest didn't want to be outdone and he jumps up and exclaims, "I caught that son of a bitch!"

For a Great Fishermen Who Has Everything by Bruce Miller and Team Golfwell

The nun that cleaned it jumps up and says, "I cleaned that son of a bitch!"

Well, the other nun didn't want to be left out and she jumps up and says, "And I baked that son of a bitch!"

Upon hearing this the pope looks around and says with a loud voice, "You know what? You motherf#%&ers are alright."

If fishing were easy, it would be called "Catching."

Fifteen best times to go fishing.

- When you need to chill out
- When you need some excitement
- When you want to be alone
- When you want to hang out with others
- When you need a little fresh air
- When you need a little exercise
- When you want to relax
- When you want to be challenged
- When you want to connect with nature
- When you need to conquer nature
- When you have a day off work
- When you don't have the day off work
- When you're a kid
- When you can take your kids
- Anytime the fish are biting.

For a Great Fishermen Who Has Everything by Bruce Miller and Team Golfwell

Life and fishing are pretty much the same things. You never know what's at the end of the line.

Sharing. Sharing the fun of fishing turns strangers into friends in a few hours.

A Fisherman's Prayer

>I pray that I might live to fish
>
>Until my dying day.
>
>And when it comes to my last cast
>
>I most humbly pray:
>
>When in the Lord's net
>
>And peacefully asleep,
>
>That in His mercy I be judged
>
>Big enough to keep.
>
>-- Breton

For a Great Fishermen Who Has Everything by Bruce Miller and Team Golfwell

For a Great Fishermen Who Has Everything by Bruce Miller and Team Golfwell

Index to paragraphs

Time well spent 1

Fisherman's prayer 1

Don't watch me! 1

A Hobby? 2

Catch a fish 2

Did you know fish can remember musical tunes? 2

I told my wife I had to stop at the bank. 3

Catfish noodling 3

Doctor. 4

Tangled lines. 4

"Give a man a fish 4

The best conversation 4

Cutting the grass or fishing? 5

Give a man a fish 5

Remembering Ted Williams 5

New at ice fishing 5

Cuban terrace 6

Roosterfish 6

For a Great Fishermen Who Has Everything by Bruce Miller and Team Golfwell

Old fish 7

Fish not biting 8

World's oldest goldfish 8

Save the goldfish! 8

When he's not talking football… 9

No eyelids 9

Obvious 9

Political discussion 10

No deduction 13

Small rod big fish story 13

Only objective 14

How small was it? 14

Liars? 15

When you gotta go 15

Ten Trivial Fish Facts 16

A connection 16

Amazing things inside fish 17

More than catching fish 18

Trout tickling 18

For a Great Fishermen Who Has Everything by Bruce Miller and Team Golfwell

Honest? 19

How can this be? 19

Being an optimist 19

Vice versa 19

Fine line 20

End to a means 20

Golden rule 20

Rays can be troublesome 20

Snapped the rod – the one that didn't get away 20

3 words 21

Bull sharks 21

Old fashioned 22

Did you know fish communicate with each other 22

Fishing dad jokes (for sharing with kids or grandkids) 22

Flashlight 27

Demagogue 28

Finding yourself 28

Definition of an angler. 28

Chumming around the world and fish tastebuds 29

Fish are like women in a way.. 30

Puzzling 30

Old sayings 30

An elusive pursuit 31

Bait (just joking). 31

More than fish 31

Did you know how fish detect movement?............................ 31

Fish or talk 32

Drone fishing 32

Important.. 33

Thirsty snake.. 33

Why did I make movies? 33

Unbelievable 34

Evening prayer 34

Dad fish joke 34

Grandpa's experience.. 35

Fishing vs. Women. 35

"I fish because I love to 35

Tigerfish tournament... 36

For a Great Fishermen Who Has Everything by Bruce Miller and Team Golfwell

Fish on! 37

Grandpa's influence 37

Fish shop 37

Getting warm 38

Father shark teaches 38

Silence is golden 39

"You can spend a lifetime at sea 39

Fish poem 39

Smallest fish in the world 40

More dad/grandpa jokes 40

Nature of Angling 42

Definition of a fish 42

Excuse me 42

Born again 43

I miss my boat 44

More dad/granddad jokes 44

Tiger 45

"Give a man a fish 45

The Most Interesting Fisherman in the World 46

Fishing license 46

Do fish sleep or just rest? 47

More dad/grandad jokes for kids. 47

The rutabaga and banana 52

Last joke not funny? Here's another. 53

Stiff 54

Water is the most essential thing on earth 55

Skishing 55

Money cannot buy happiness 56

Just an ordinary commoner 56

Fishing docks 56

Three things to tell the wife you are going fishing 56

Excuses when you don't catch fish. 57

Large lettering on the back of your favorite fishing vest: 58

Angler 58

Worry 58

Teach fishing 59

Fishing poem 59

An old one 59

Double win 60

Did you know? 60

Sunday school 61

Respecting privacy 61

Skarping 61

Crazy Baits 62

I only fish 63

Girls who like fishing 63

Braggart 63

Pacific Hagfish 64

Hard work and luck 64

Women puzzle over this 64

Speedy sailfish 64

Finding new places 64

The right bait 65

Convincing the wife 65

Lesson in History 66

Fly rod 67

A fishing fable for kids or grandkids 67

Finding peace. 68

Fishing guides 68

Fishing trip 69

A delusion 69

Pants on fire 69

A simple and wonderful woman 70

Thanks, dad 70

No fisherman? 70

Surprise rescue 71

Give a man a fish and he'll eat for a day 72

Addicted 72

Racoon swordfish story 73

African Remora fishing 74

When in Rome 74

Unwelcome surprise 74

Good question 75

Taste 76

Phone in the lake 76

Therapy 76

For a Great Fishermen Who Has Everything by Bruce Miller and Team Golfwell

Q. What's the difference 76

Outdoors 76

An old one you might have heard 77

Time for fishing 77

Needs a second opinion 78

Ocean City Maryland and Cabo San Lucas here I come! 78

The memory of a fish 79

Thinking and fishing 79

Not perfect 80

From birth to death 80

All kinds of fishing tournaments. 80

Born to sell 81

The one that got away 82

Sounds 83

Love to fish 84

Indecent 84

Another big fish story. 84

Expensive 85

On tour 85

From a woman's perspective 86

Catching a fish with a snake 86

Getting off the couch 86

Thanks wife! 86

The largest fish ever caught 87

All-Star game v. Fishing 87

Did you know fish help each other? 88

Simple 88

Refreshments 88

IGFA World Records 88

Acting 89

Relief 89

Charter captain and the IRS 89

Boat Owner 90

Don't bother me 90

Alone with nature 90

Love seafood 90

The Pope 91

Want to go fishing? 92

For a Great Fishermen Who Has Everything by Bruce Miller and Team Golfwell

Smell the roses 92

Fill it up.. 92

Like sex 93

Born to fish 93

Old fisherman saying 93

Fishing for speeders 94

All sizes... 94

Knock-Knock 94

A woman's view 95

Fly fishermen 96

Mark the spot 96

Beauty 96

Fish aren't dumb 96

Definition of a fish 97

Holy water... 97

Three blondes.. 97

Horseback Trawling.. 98

Once I retire and slow down 99

How can you tell hold old a fish is?................................ 99

Good things 99

Negotiate 99

One thing 100

It's the clothes 100

Secret fishing spot 100

Priest catches a big fish 100

If fishing were easy 102

Fifteen best times to go fishing. 102

Life and fishing are pretty much the same things 103

Sharing. 103

A Fisherman's Prayer 103

We hope you enjoyed our book! 117

About the authors 118

Bruce Miller 118

TeamGolfwell 118

We Want to Hear from You! 119

Other Books by Bruce Miller and Team Golfwell 120

Index to paragraphs 121

For a Great Fishermen Who Has Everything by Bruce Miller and Team Golfwell

We hope you enjoyed our book!

If you liked our book, we would sincerely appreciate your taking a few moments to leave a brief review.

Thank you again very much!

TeamGolfwell and Bruce Miller

Bruce@TeamGolfwell.com

For a Great Fishermen Who Has Everything by Bruce Miller and Team Golfwell

About the authors

Bruce Miller. Lawyer, businessman, world traveler, golf enthusiast, Golf Rules Official, actor, whiskey connoisseur, and author of over 40 books, a few being Amazon bestsellers, spends his days writing, studying, and constantly learning of the astounding, unexpected, and amazing events happening in the world today while exploring the brighter side of life. He is a member of Team Golfwell, Authors, and Publishers.

TeamGolfwell are bestselling authors and founders of the very popular 230,000+ member Facebook Group "Golf Jokes and Stories." Their books have sold thousands of copies including several #1 bestsellers in Golf Coaching, Sports humor, and other categories.

We Want to Hear from You!

"There usually is a way to do things better and there is opportunity when you find it." - Thomas Edison

We love to hear your thoughts and suggestions on anything and please feel free to contact us at
Bruce@TeamGolfwell.com

For a Great Fishermen Who Has Everything by Bruce Miller and Team Golfwell

Other Books by Bruce Miller [55] and Team Golfwell [56]

Brilliant Screen-Free Stuff to Do with Kids: A Handy Reference for Parents & Grandparents!

For the Golfer Who Has Everything: A Funny Golf Book

For the Mother Who Has Everything: A Funny Book for Mother

For the Father Who Has Everything: A Funny Book for Father

For the Grandmother Who Has Everything: A Funny Book for Grandmothers

For the Grandfather Who Has Everything: A Funny Book for Grandfathers

The Funniest Quotations to Brighten Every Day: Brilliant, Inspiring, and Hilarious Thoughts from Great Minds

Jokes for Very Funny Kids (Ages 3 to 7): Funny Jokes, Riddles and More

Jokes for Very Funny Kids (Big & Little): Funny Jokes and Riddles Ages 9 - 12 and up and many more. [57]

For a Great Fishermen Who Has Everything by Bruce Miller and Team Golfwell

Index to paragraphs

---

[1] Supra. SPCA
[2] Wikipedia, Noodling, https://en.wikipedia.org/wiki/Noodling
[3] Ibid.
[4] Oceana, https://oceana.org/marine-life/orange-roughy/
[5] Ibid.
[6] Daily Mail, https://www.dailymail.co.uk/news/article-1262250/Great-grandmother-tagged-selling-goldfish.html
[7] Cousteau.org. https://www.cousteau.org/news/why-dont-fish-have-eyelids/
[8] For the Win, USA Today, https://ftw.usatoday.com/2018/10/giant-blue-marlin-caught-on-light-tackle-is-a-pending-world-record
[9] Ibid.
[10] Odditycentral, https://www.odditycentral.com/news/microfishing-when-the-tiniest-fish-becomes-the-biggest-catch.html
[11] Ibid.
[12] Wikipedia, Trout tickling, https://en.wikipedia.org/wiki/Trout_tickling
[13] Ibid.
[14] Daily Mail, https://www.dailymail.co.uk/news/article-1153982/World-record-British-angler-lands-55-stone-stingray-thats-FIVE-TIMES-weight.html
[15] Scientific American, https://blogs.scientificamerican.com/science-sushi/mythbusting-101-bulking-up-with-bull-shark-testosterone/
[16] Naples Daily News, https://archive.naplesnews.com/news/local/shark-bite-sinks-boat-100-miles-off-fort-myers-beach-ep-404915160-345658762.html/
[17] SPCA, https://spca.bc.ca/news/fun-facts-about-fish/
[18] Wikipedia, https://en.wikipedia.org/wiki/Chumming
[19] Parker, Steve. Angelfish, Megamouth Sharks, & Other Fish (Animal Kingdom Classification). Minneapolis, MN: David West Children's Book, 2005.
[20] Supra. SPCA

[21] Herald Zimbabwe, https://www.herald.co.zw/all-set-for-tiger-tournament/
[22] Ibid.
[23] Fish (Eyewitness Books). New York, NY: Dorling Kindersley Limited, 2005.
[24] NOAA, supra.
[25] Wikipedia, https://en.wikipedia.org/wiki/Dwarf_pygmy_goby#
[26] Britannica Illustrated Science Library. Fish and Amphibians. Chicago, IL: Encyclopedia Britannica, Inc, 2008.
[27] NOAA, supra.
[28] Wikipedia, Skishing, https://en.wikipedia.org/wiki/Skishing
[29] Ibid.
[30] NOAA, supra.
[31] Head, Honor. Amazing Fish (Amazing Life Cycles). Pleasantville, NY: Gareth Stevens Publishing, 2008.
[32] Ibid.
[33] "Skarping" YouTube, https://www.youtube.com/watch?v=uqykDINEcGo
[34] Farmer's Almanac, https://www.farmersalmanac.com/fishing-bait-124898
[35] Ibid.
[36] Wikipedia, Hagfish, https://en.wikipedia.org/wiki/Hagfish#Slime
[37] White Marlin Open, https://whitemarlinopen.com/
[38] Bisbee Black and Blue Marlin Tournament, https://www.haciendacaboresort.com/things-to-do/bisbee-black-and-blue-marlin-tournament
[39] Midcurrent, https://midcurrent.com/science/fish-eyesight-does-color-matter/
[40] Science Daily, https://www.sciencedaily.com/releases/2014/07/140701193253.htm#:
[41] Lake County banner, https://lakecountybanner.com/different-types-of-fishing-tournaments-for-every-angler/
[42] Ibid.
[43] Ibid.
[44] Supra, Britannica Illustrated Science Library.

[45] YouTube, Catching fish with a snake, https://calsportsmanmag.com/insane-fishing-technique-snake-is-the-angler/
[46] Ibid. YouTube is at https://youtu.be/XDS2WWg9eZ4
[47] HMY.com, https://www.hmy.com/biggest-fish-ever-caught/#:~:text=According%20to%20IGFA%20records%2C%20the,against%20this%20one%2Dton%20shark.
[48] Instagram.com, https://www.instagram.com/p/BXEZQeXD_H9/?utm_source=ig_embed&ig_rid=bc65ac88-511c-4e80-9f06-a207b87532a1
[49] Supra.
[50] Supra. SPCA
[51] https://igfa.org/igfa-world-records-search/.
[52] Ibid.
[53] Ibid.
[54] NOAA, supra.
[55] https://www.amazon.com/Bruce-Miller/e/B096C9SN2R?
[56] https://www.amazon.com/Team-Golfwell/e/B01CFW4EQG?
[57] Ibid.

Milton Keynes UK
Ingram Content Group UK Ltd.
UKHW020621081224
3499UKWH00005B/13

9 781991 164100